A PRIME ENTERTAINER'S SURVIVAL GUIDE:

Lessons So Far

By

Cynthia Harris Tademy

Prime: *adjective* 1. Of the first importance; demanding the fullest consideration; *noun* 1. The most flourishing stage or state.

Entertainer: 1. a professional singer, comedian or other performer who takes part in public entertainment; 2. a person who entertains.

Prime Entertainer: 1. An older, mature professional (or amateur) actor, singer, comedian or other performer who takes part in public entertainments; 2. An older, mature person who likes entertaining an audience, fulfilling a lifelong dream.

- Cynthia Harris Tademy

TABLE OF CONTENTS

Introduction   7

Desire/Skill/Talent   10

Family: They Gotta Love You!   13

Keep Your Day Job/Get One   17

Agents/Managers/Independent Contracting

                                       27

Marketing   43

Auditioning   69

Rejection   81

Training   84

Money Matters   88

Scams   93

Talk Story   97

The Last Word   120

Acknowledgements   123

Hampton Roads, VA Places of Interest

126

Index   131

    Ex. 1-Headshots   132
    Ex. 2-Resume   134
    Ex. 3-Technical Resume   135
    Ex. 4-Business Cards   136
    Ex. 5-Tools of the Trade   137
    Ex. 6-Websites and Social Media
                                          138
    Ex.7-Local Hangouts   140
    Ex.8-Colleges and Universities
                                          146
    Ex. 9-Photographers   147

Recommended Books   149

Biography   151

INTRODUCTION

I was so ready to start a new life. I had retired from the United States Navy with a total of 25.5 years of combined Active and Reserve time. I had wanted to be a REAL actor for a long, long time.

There had been an attempt when I was in my 20s. Unfocused, scared and very impressionably living in Los Angeles, I thought I would be the next big singer and actor. I even met some people whose careers whooshed by me, rising like Danny

Glover or slowing like Phillip Michael Thomas.[1]

So here I was, culminating a military career, and still dreaming of being an actor. This book is the marker of my journey so far. It is not the ultimate how-to; it is probably only apropos to my present living area, the Hampton Roads area of Virginia. Yet, I have been asked how I developed my career and promoted myself. My target audience are those of my own age, the late bloomers of the Baby Boomer Generation.

---

[1] With all due respect, I do not know these men personally nor do I know what they are doing now. This time period was 1980-1985 and my encounters with them were brief and unmemorable to them.

Nevertheless, if you young people can gain some wisdom from my journey, "it is well with my soul."

These are the lessons so far.

Cynthia H. Tademy

DESIRE/SKILL/TALENT – Even Now

At this age – What CAN you do? What are you still doing? Singing? Acting? Dancing? Telling jokes? Juggling? Turning flips? Playing an instrument?

This may be the book's shortest chapter because I'm going to assume there is something you can do that makes you get in front of total strangers and risk making a complete fool of yourself. Nevertheless, here are the questions.

Is it a desire? A wish or desire but something you have never done or tried or probably will never make yourself do. Not enough.

Is it a skill? Did you begin to take lessons at an early age and you are now more than proficient at what you do? Have you passed your teacher's level and have that need to show the world? You may have something.

Is it a natural talent? You come from a family of guitar players and you play the fiddle very well. Or your friends invite you to every party because they know your life observations will keep everybody laughing for hours. There *is* something there.

But wait! You're 32 to 48. You're raising a family; in the middle of a good career. No, you're 49 to 62. The kids are gone; you've downsized. You just retired or even resigned because you've had enough. No, you're 65. You don't want to have to work, but you're bored. Maybe you'll take this singing from a karaoke hobby to something different, like getting paid to sing …

Whatever it is inside – desire, skill or raw talent – all you know is that you have to try it. Whether it is your first attempt, or you tried before and you have to try again before you die. You are going to be an entertainer. You are ready for the next step.

FAMILY: They gotta love you!

Here is hoping that you have the perfect spouse, perfect children. They cheer you on to every audition. They help carpool to every rehearsal, bringing you lunch or keeping dinner ready when you get home. Your spouse is the perfect baby-sitter, available at the drop of a hat. On opening night, they have flowers waiting for you. They come to every performance, cheering madly when you take your bow.

You know life does not happen like this. You are blessed, if you have one of the above statements active in your life. If you decide to go professional, it will be very important that you have a support system.

You will be dealing with rejection on a regular basis. A spouse who has agreed to this career path will know how you process it, whether you need some space at home or you need to talk or cry, etc. They will be part of your plan if you need to vent; or if you get the part you want, how to celebrate your success.

Speaking of support system, you may or may not have friends who understand show business. The friends who do will try to attend your performances. Some elder friends do not EVER attend: they are in bed by 9 pm. Do not be mad at them. Your kids may not attend either, especially if they are the age where anything Mom or Dad does is embarrassing or they have their own school/social life. If your social circle has been a church, a bowling team, a book club, or a poker game, you may begin to feel some distance over time. You are doing something they do not understand. You are being braver at a time when others feel you should be slowing down. Slowing down is relative these days, as more adults are working longer. You are choosing to work in a field that makes you happy, with or without a large income.

There is the instance that you are alone. You have moved since retiring, another part of town or another part of the country. The support system may have dwindled away to nothing. This is where your inner strength has to sustain you. Get out there and make new friends from the very venues that supported you before. This time, make your circle of friends about 50/50: half performers, half regular people. It will be important that your life feels like it is balanced so you can concentrate on your craft.

KEEP YOUR DAY JOB/GET ONE

Keep your day job. Really? Really.
Unless you are retired, or have a family
fortune, stock or annuities that pay you well,
keep working. You will need a wage to
keep up your rent, your food, your
transportation, and your clothes.

Regular Work
Most regular work is 8 or 9 hours, with
no flexibility built in. It will be up to you to
find those initial hours to work your craft.
You will definitely use evening hours; use
your holiday hours, too, but carefully.
Instead of going on a vacation for fun, you
could use three or more days to go to a

17

metro-size city and audition. You can use your vacation month(s) to be in a community or regional theater production or to produce an acting showcase for yourself and for others. If you "like" your regular job, make sure your work does not suffer because nights and weekends are taken up with your craft. The day will come, sooner or later, when you will HAVE to choose between your job and your artistic endeavors. Some people keep their jobs until retirement. Save up as much money as you can until the time comes for you to change jobs or stop working all together.

Saving Money

Some of us have been great saving money for our projects through our adult lifetime: some of us – not so much. Others have had family obligations that took priority. If you do not have that stash of money, keep working or wait until you retire. Over time, you can make a small salary from your performance gigs. I am not saying you will be famous and will command a large, negotiated salary. I am saying that, over time, you can make enough money to give up full-time or continue to work part-time and make money on weekends.

Temporary Agencies

Temporary agencies are wonderful resources for short-term employment. After your chosen agency tests you to place your skills and abilities, you can negotiate what kind of job you contract to do. Whether it is 3 days, 5 weeks or 1 year, temporary jobs usually will have more flexibility of time built -in. The possibility of losing a job because of attending an audition exists, but the agency itself is your buffer. Make sure you are negotiating your immediate needs in your agency contract.

Interim Jobs

Interim jobs are working situations that are short-termed from the beginning. Whether with an independent contractor or with your city or the U.S. Government, these jobs have finite start and stop dates. For example, in 2010, I worked for the Census Bureau, which is part of the Department of Commerce. I had a clerical position that began in January 2010 and ended at the end of the big Census cycle in May. Since then, I have been contacted a second time and offered another interim position as a Census Field Representative for a smaller survey. Again, the job was for only 5 months. Yet both times, I was able to arrange my hours so that I could audition and do film work as needed.

Independent Contractor (Direct Marketing)

Are you good at selling products? Then you should definitely become an independent contractor for some type of direct marketing, such as AVON, Mary Kay, Tupperware, Discovery Toys, SMC, Scentsy, Legal Shield, Ardyss, PriAmerica Financial Services, Herbalife, Arbonne, 5LINX, Silpada Jewelry, Partylite Candles, and The Pampered Chef. The above companies are the ones that either I have participated in or attended a sales party and seen the merchandise. Or you can fashion your own home business from your skill/hobby: carpentry, sewing/crafting, cooking, babysitting, etc. Whatever you have the skill and patience to do as a business, you can do. Most independent work does NOT require a business license, but do your research. Along with acting items (to be discussed later), there can be tax benefits to having a home business and office supplies. Something else to do when you are not acting …

Part-time/Interim Jobs

It may not be easy to find part-time work: you are in competition with younger people, students, stay-at-home partners, other older seniors or immigrants. At this writing, there has been a long recession, and EVERYONE wants work. Ironically, most of the country has been living like a "starving artist." The difference will be as the economy improves, you CHOOSE to stay in this lower economic position.

The typical jobs are fast food, office/clerical, seasonal retail, light construction, recreational-vacation work, food service and childcare. These are all fine, as long as the hours are flexible and you enjoy the work. However, if you are not physically able to do those types of jobs, do not waste your time applying for them. They can also be mentally demeaning, especially if you retired from middle management or higher.

Keep your options open for the unusual. For example: every 10 years, the U.S. Census Bureau, under the Department of Commerce, hires hundreds of civilian and retired military for the National Census. They also conduct smaller surveys in between the Centennial Census. These openings are typically 3-, 4-, to 6-month jobs. The Federal Government has several of these interim positions available under various other departments and offices; research will be necessary to find them under websites such as www.usajobs.gov, the various city/state web pages, www.amerijob.com, www.monster.com, www.opm.gov, etc. Just put "government jobs" or "part-time government jobs" in a search engine like GOGGLE, and research what you are looking for.

Be careful. Be honest with yourself. If you find the job that has just enough money and the flexible hours you need, but you turn out to be a whiz, you may be offered full-time employment. If you find you enjoy the job, the people and the environment, then perhaps acting/singing needs to go back to being a hobby. Only YOU know what will work for you. Either way, be happy; be at peace with your choices.

AGENTS/MANAGERS/INDEPENDENT CONTRACTING

Agents

In Hampton Roads, you can meet an agent a number of ways. You might be doing a community theater play; the agent approaches you, with a business card, after the show. You may have heard a particular name several times in conversation and decide to investigate by looking up that person's website. A friend or associate maybe refer you or actually introduce you at a party. In the past few years, networking parties have been arranged by organizations such as the Virginia Production Alliance, or by professional event planners like Hampton Roads to Hollywood.com.

If you are taking lessons at an acting school, your instructor can arrange a showcase at the end of the semester or the school cycle. Of course, if YOU are the planner among your friends, you can produce your own showcase by renting the venue, contracting your concessions, tickets, and the publicity. Some will be good at this, having done this type of event planning or programming in their civilian work career.

An agent gets you your paying gigs or work. He/she receives breakdowns or casting notices from clients and match up the roles to their talent roster. They receive 10 to 15% of the actor's fee. NOTE: please be aware of the agent's roster of talent. They are going to send out the people they think are best for the CLIENT'S needs. Sometimes you will be sent out, solo, because you are the person the agent feels best suited for that role or gig; other times you will go out with a few of your type, scheduled at separate times. If you think

that you need more attention or you begin to
get more requests/referrals for work, then
you might be ready for a manager.

Managers

A manager will be working for you
exclusively, but be careful: you must pay an
additional 10, 15, or 20% of your check.
Managers are your employees that you hire
and pay; you CONTRACT with an agent,
who takes their cut, then pays you. NEVER
pay agents or managers money upfront: a
sure sign of a scam. Some actors sign

exclusivity contracts with their talent
agencies or with their studios; this is your
choice. But make sure you get legal counsel
and understand whether you need this or not.
You may be so eager to sign a contract that
you find yourself bound indefinitely with an
agency: it may take years or a large amount
of money to legally break. And don't forget
to pay your lawyer and your accountant!

Independent Contracting

Actors will occasionally find their own work; that makes them an independent contractor or self-employed. There are callboards, electronic bulletin boards, notices, emails and ads that an actor can receive from various sources for work. The advent of the Internet has made it easy to research venues on your own. Casting directors may contact you directly and ask your availability (time). Be honest: if you are not available or you have contracted with another project, say so up-front. The requesting party will either work with you or tell you if this option is non-negotiable. There is more respect gained by saying **<u>no</u>** to a project than to accept it and miss it because you over-scheduled yourself.

Negotiation

I suggest meeting with your agent regularly to negotiate your working relationship. Some actors are so intent on the work that they do not pay attention to this. Like a good marriage, how the actor and his/her agent work together is important.

Talk about your day job, your family and how much time the agent can spend on you. For some of you, this is a complete career change. You want to spend as much time planning your time now as you learned to do in your first career. Know how your agent works: the office hours, the staff, the percentage cut, and the roster of talent. Be familiar with the agent's website, for oftentimes, this is where the client first sees your headshot. Is the website professional looking? Is it easy to access and understand? If you have your own website, are you able to connect with theirs? Can

you afford your own site? Find out what the

net arrangement (money pay out) is between

the agent and the client. How and when will

you be paid? How often should you see or

visit your agent's office? Does your agent

attend or view your work? Is it ok if you

accept work from a different agent? These

are the important questions that should be

asked. Young people are often intimidated

with their agent because of the maturity of

the agent or the length of time the agent has

been in the business or by the agent's

personality. As an older actor, these should not be the reasons you do not understand how the agent conducts business with YOU. If there is contention or misunderstandings between you that go unresolved too long, you need to find another agent, one that fits your personality better.

LISTINGS

Hutson Talent Agency
39 Burtis Street
Portsmouth, VA 23702
(757) 673-6436

Stevenson's Modeling Agency
P.O. Box 55456
Virginia Beach, VA 23471
(757) 481-7330

Central Casting
623 Pennsylvania Ave Southeast
Washington, DC 20003
(202) 547-6300

The Chez Group
2221 Peachtree Road Northeast
Atlanta, GA 30309-1148
(404) 603-8755

Studio Center
5245 Cleveland St # 204
Virginia Beach, VA 23462-6505
(757) 420-3605

Pat Moran and Associates
3500 Boston Street Suite 425
Baltimore, MD 21224

Taylor Royall Casting
6247 Falls Road
Baltimore, MD 21209
(410) 828-6900

Corrigan & Johnston Casting
3006 North Davidson Street
Charlotte, NC 28205-1042
(704) 374-9400

JTA, Inc.
820 E. Boulevard
Charlotte, NC 28203-5116
(704) 377-5987

The Brock Agency
329 13th Avenue NW
Hickory, NC 28601
(828) 322-8553

Finncannon Casting
1235 23rd Street North
Wilmington, NC 28405-1809
(910) 251-1500

Maultsby Talent
Landfall Executive Suites
1213 Culbreth Drive
Wilmington, NC 28405
(910) 509-4008 / (877) 490-0006

MJM Talent
2011 Carolina Beach Road
Wilmington, NC 28401-7201
(910) 251-3734

Heery Casting
2618-22 E. Cumberland Street
 Philadelphia, PA 19125
(215) 238-9240

Mike Lemon Casting
413 N. 7th Street
Philadelphia. PA 19123
(215) 627-8927

Carlyn Davis Casting
124 E. Broad Street Unit C-2
Falls Church, VA 22046
(703) 532-1900

Talent Link
8907 Watlington Rd
Richmond, VA 23229
(804) 562-1878

Uptown Talent, Inc.
1129 Gaskins Road #202
Richmond, VA 23233
(804) 740-0307

MODELOGIC [WILHELMINA]
2501 E. Broad Street
Richmond, VA 23223 2501
(804) 644-1000

Jaderlund Casting
4410 E. Claiborne Street Suite 334
Hampton, Virginia 23666
(505) 552-2867

Erica Arvold Casting
416 E. Main St
Suite 206
Charlottesville, VA 22902
Tel: (434) 878-0804

MARKETING

You should realize, as an actor, YOU are your best product in your own home business. When you walk into an audition, you are saying that you are the best candidate to portray a character, represent a product, or a client's other creative business interests. You are in a profession that has always been competitive and fickle. Show business is competitive because the supply of players is ALWAYS more than the demand or needs of the clients. It is a BUSINESS, just like the career you just left. By keeping your personal feelings in check (just like you did at work), you should use all the tools available to present yourself in a positive manner.

Your first important tool is your headshot (Example 1). A headshot or HS is an 8" x 10" color photograph of you, taken from approximately chest up, with the focus on your face. Your headshot should look like you NOW: not 15 years ago; not a glamorous, re-touched snapshot or family portrait. Often film work as an extra depends on how you look in context to the director's vision. Adjustments to your appearance can be made with costuming and makeup. Look for local photographers who specialize in headshots (Example 9). They sometimes offer a package deal of one or two "looks" on a CD that you can use to reproduce multiple copies of your headshot. The photographer will also give you a release letter that allows you to reproduce your pictures (yes, you paid for them, but the photographer is protecting his/her work). Make sure that you have 5 or 10 physical headshots available at all times. I keep 2-4 HS on file in my house and have provided my primary agent with a HS CD so she can digitally provide a copy to a client at anytime (this is a personal arrangement I have with just one of my agents). One good picture is usually all that is needed, however, if you have a particular look you want to emphasize, then have that look also

(evil villain, soccer mom, femme fatale, etc.)

The average cost for 1 look (as of 2011) is

$75 - $150. Some photographers offer

makeup for the shot or provide a stylist for

an additional fee. Multiple packages or

bundles can run $280 - $1,200. The best

thing to do with your best shot is to

reproduce it multiple times. A good supply

is 50 – 100 copies. If you move to a

metropolitan area, 100 to 300 copies is a

good number. Some actors do mail-outs to

agents and casting agencies on a regular

basis, so a good inventory is necessary.

There are special, large 8.5 x 10.5 envelopes

available with a clear plastic backing on

them so agents and casting staff can quickly

see your shots before opening them. One

source for these HS envelopes is

www.theactorsphotolab.com or through

www.amazon.com. Multiple copies can be

ordered through the photographer; photo

websites like www.snapfish.com,

www.reproductions.com ; and through

pharmacy photo shops like

www.walgreens.com or www.riteaid.com .

Whenever I update my headshot, I process a

copy through my pharmacy website, who

then stores it. This way, when I need a fast

copy, I can go online and order it overnight,

for pick-up the next day. I also keep copies

of various sizes and looks on file on my

computer, so I can attach a headshot to a

casting/audition email.

The next important tool is your resume

(Example 2). This text document differs in

style from your work resume: it lists your

performances in chronological order, and by

medium. The resume should be printed on

8" x 10" paper so that you can staple it on

the back of your headshot. A regular sheet,

8.5" x 11," tacked on a headshot, looks

slovenly and unprofessional. 8" x 10" paper

can be purchased by the ream or cut for you

at your favorite copy shop. Some actors glue their resumes on their headshots, most staple it. The idea is to keep them together and portable: they will be filed in a drawer, in a folder, on the wall or mailed in a group. Never lie to fill up your acting resume: it is better to be known for a few good films or plays than to list material you have not performed. In small markets, there is always someone who can verify whether you were actually involved or not.

Production crews also keep resumes (Example 3). Crew member's duties and skills are often interchangeable so keeping a tech resume is important, especially non-union members. It is a way of getting credit for various works done on various projects until a chosen skill is developed. Once that skill is chosen, the crew member can apply the credits to the appropriate union's membership requirements.

Another important tool is a business card. Because you never know when you will meet someone influential, carry them everywhere. Give them out freely, especially when your conversation is about your career. I not only give them out in casual conversation, but also on set, in rehearsal or at the end of the day. On set, I pass them to as many cast and crew as possible. Some of the best acting opportunities are referrals from people I have worked with in the past. Your business card is information on how to get in touch with you (Example 4). Your acting name, address, phone number and email are the basics. If you do not want to include your personal phone number, then provide your agent's number, email and website. Business cards may have different designs on them that portray your favorite medium (film strips, cameras, drama masks, lights, etc.) or may have a miniature of your headshot. The cards are inexpensive. With your computer you may make your own, order them from a printing source like www.officemax.com , www.vistaprint.com, order them from an established local printer or from some HS photographers. Crew members sometimes style their cards in the shapes of their craft, such as ladders, hanging lights, and lipstick cases. Along with business cards, you can design postcards and thank-you cards. The postcards allow you to publicize your events and performances; the thank-you cards are a personal way to show gratitude for the audition or the referral. Mail your thank-you cards immediately after your audition, the next day or after your wrap party: set yourself apart by showing old-fashioned appreciation.

The headshot, resume and business cards

are your basic marketing tools; other items are optional. Keep track of your contacts, auditions and "booked" work in a file or log. You can make your first log with a notebook or by using any office software, such as Microsoft WORD, EXCEL or ACCESS. There are printed log books made for your special category: actor, model, musician, etc. I use a log called The Organized Actor by Leslie Becker, purchased online from www.OrganizedActor.com. Not only is it a log, but a receipt book, address/contact list, and career planner. Another good planner can be obtained from www.holdonlog.com. These log books can be purchased for actors, models, young actors, background artists, live performers and voice-over artists. This site also links to an online log product called www.PerformerTrack.com that can be subscribed to monthly. There is no wrong way to do this, it is purely personal preference: by this printing, there are smartphone applications for tracking auditions and rehearsing lines!

One of the tools trending now is having a personal website or an account/fan page on a social website. It can be a simple one, but it basically puts the first three tools on full display. It also allows you to have a central place for ALL of your tools, including a demo reel. A demonstration or demo reel is a video recording of you acting out a scene, a monologue or a commercial. It can be a collection of small scenes or one longer scene that is well-done. The reel should not be longer than 3 to 8 minutes because agents and casting directors do not always watch them longer than that. With their experience, they can determine if you are right for the part they are casting within the first 3 minutes. Some photographers are also videographers and can include your demo reel in your headshot package. Videographers advertise their packages from $150 up. Please make sure your reel looks as professional as possible. As much as your family wants to help you, if they are not professional camera people who shoot, edit and finish your reel, the people you are trying to impress to hire you will NOT take you seriously. Why? If you do not care enough to present yourself professionally, they will not care to pay you for shoddy work or invest their money in their creative BUSINESS efforts.

Know Your Type and Age Range

There will be the naysayer (haters) who will tell you, "You are too old for that." If you know your type, you will know whether

you can get work or not. Hollywood will

always attract the young and the beautiful,

but someone has to play other adults,

looking natural and authentic. Those roles

are counselors, teachers, executives,

supervisors; grandparents, elderly patients

and insurance recipients. Because these

roles need to be realistic, you do not have to

go to Hollywood to audition.

Communication media, public relation and

human resource agencies hire locally to

meet corporate need.

Type

You are a 5' white female, a little plump,

American apple pie cute. You can play a

neighbor, a nurse, a school crossing guard.

You are a 5'10 African American man, thin-

framed, a faded cut over your eyebrow. You

can play a firefighter, a construction

surveyor, a football coach. Grey hair? You

will make an interesting doctor, lawyer, or

realtor. Big feet? Sell shoes, podiatry

products or a massage client. Beautifully

shaped, but age-spotted hands? Sell lotions,

cover make-up, gloves, medicinal creams

and ointments. Your agent, acting teacher, career coach or manager will help you identify your strong points.

Age

You can and should be proud of your mature years, your prime. Again, the young people are not interested in playing too old an age (unless they have been trained in universities or conservatories). You can proudly display your lines and wrinkles in everything: films, television, commercials, industrial and training videos. For instance, re-enactors of historical drama prefer people who have strong, identifiable regional features. There will be people who will consider plastic surgery: this is a personal choice. The West Coast has a high percentage of actors who choose to accentuate and/or change their features. It is NOT a guarantee for employment. Again, this will be a PERSONAL choice. Like your civilian work resume, you do not HAVE to list your actual age. I often list myself as "mature," "older actor," even "senior citizen," depending on the audition.

Wardrobe

You have got years worth of clothes;
what a great position to be in! You have
booked an industrial/training video and your
agent tells you to wear business casual.
Business casual clothes are the items in your
closet that you have worn to work for years:
unstructured and regular suits, pantsuits,
twin sets, sports coats, casual shirts,
sweaters, casual slacks and pants. You will
need to decide how much to keep, but do not
give all away. Some film and theatrical
productions look for clothes from a specific

time, like the 60's or the 40's, or uniforms from past foreign wars. In addition, if you still can fit them, you should keep them.

Another good thing about clothes is being able to donate them during tax season. Good, clean clothes not wanted are donated to Goodwill or Disabled Veterans or The Salvation Army. They can also be donated directly to various theaters, school wardrobe closets, and costume departments. This is also an excellent source for period clothing for yourself, particularly if you are interested in reenactments.

So you have your agent, your acting tools and your marketing plan together. Are you ready to go out there and get some work? On your mark … get set … Go AUDITION!

AUDITIONING

Be on time. Remember when you use to get ready for school the night before? Laying out your clothes and gathering everything for your book bag by the door? This is still a good practice to use the night before an audition. Along with the before mentioned tools, have an Actor's Bag in your car at all times (Example 5). You will be less nervous knowing you did not forget any of your "equipment and tools." Map out where you are going the night before. Whether you use your GPS, "Google©,"

"Yahoo©," or a fold-out paper map, KNOW

where you are going. Whenever possible,

get there 15 or 20 minutes before your

appointed time. If you are a natural late

morning sleeper, schedule afternoon

sessions. I schedule afternoon sessions

when I drive to Richmond, VA because the

city's commuter traffic can be unpredictable

during peak work hours. If audition sides

(dialogue) have been provided, practice

speaking them during the drive. I factor in a

rest stop at a VA Visitors Center, about 13

miles outside of Richmond, so that I can

freshen up or change clothes. On the occasion that the audition is further than Richmond, ask your agent if anyone else is going and consider a carpool. NOTE: do not carpool with another actor for the same part. Camaraderie is good in its place, but this can cause extreme anxiety for both parties. It can ruin good friendships and fracture poor ones. It can also make you second guess your performance, no matter how prepared you are. There are some actors who will try to sabotage your ability because they are auditioning for the same part. After all, it IS a competition. As you become more experienced at YOUR audition process, you will know whether or not you can handle the carpooling situation or not.

80% of your job as an actor is auditioning! Develop a strong confidence about this part of your career; at least know how to project that attitude. Remember those relaxation exercises your acting teacher/coach taught you? This is where you use them! Becoming calm and centered helps you remember your sides, your memorized monologues, keep your body

fresh and helps you concentrate when you

work with a partner. Allow your personality

to show as naturally as possible; remember –

they WANT to see you.

You have arrived at your audition. Turn

off your cell phone or smartphone. Lock up

your iPad©, notebook, or laptop in your car.

A good habit to have is to assume your

confidence as you exit your car. Take those

deep breaths as you enter the building. Be

pleasant to the receptionist or production

assistant who guides you to your waiting

area. Sign in and prepare your HS/resume

to turn in. Some auditions will assign you a

number and take an additional photo of you.

Find a chair or a space in the room and read

over what is required. In some auditions,

you will know no one in the room; other

times, you will know everyone in the room.

Smile, nod, wave and occasionally hug the

nearest person to you (if that is your

personality) but remember: you are there to

get a JOB, not have a party. Some auditions

will feel like a noisy coffeehouse; others

will feel like a court room. Be observant to

the climate the production team is providing and act accordingly. If you need fresh air or the bathroom or even a smoke out of the building, let the assistant know where you are AT ALL TIMES. You may be needed for an additional audition as a scene partner or to be matched for costume considerations. If you leave the area, the team WILL assume you are finished and no longer interested in participating! You do not have to chat up the assistant; they have a job to do keeping the audition organized. Do not be rude. Yet, if you have a question, ask it before you are seen. Be remembered not only for being a good actor, but handling yourself in a professional manner.

You have just completed your audition. If a hand is offered, shake it; otherwise say thank you and exit the room. Return the sides to the assistant (if necessary) and say thank you again. If there are business cards on the sign-in table, take one and leave one of yours. Look around the room to make sure you are not leaving any of your personal things, and leave. Again, carry that confidence all the way to your vehicle.

Now, breathe. Again. Again. Relax.

You did it! Now it is natural to review in
your head everything you just did, but be
careful not to beat yourself up if you think
you made mistakes. Auditioning takes
practice, too. The more you do it, the better
you handle it. Are you suddenly hungry?
Drive to the nearest eating place and eat. If
you have the time, get out of your car and
dine-in. Turn your cell back on.
Sometimes I call my agent, especially if a

compliment has been given by the casting director. Another reason to turn the phone back on after the audition is to be available for immediate callback. It does happen, especially at the end of the work day. If the production crew knows you are from out-of-town, you may be called back, soon after you leave, to be matched up to a different partner or re-considered for an additional role.

So now what? You wait. Develop a routine for HOW you wait on that call. Drive back to town, rocking out to your music in your

car. Go for a run; go to a movie. Go hang
out with non-industry friends. If you are
tired, take a nap. Continue to "decompress"
from that energy level. Write out a thank
you card and mail it the same day. Or send
an email that says thank you for the audition
and ONLY THAT.

REJECTION

Your agent calls. You did not get the part. How do you deal with rejection? At this mature stage of your life, you should have some coping mechanisms in place for dealing with rejection. As part of your new acting career, well, it will hurt a little and it may call for some new habits. First, DO NOT CALL the casting team and ask them why. It is unprofessional and it will be a long, LONG time before you hear from that group if you do. If you need a face-to-face discussion, make an appointment with your agent instead. Let the agent give you feedback on what your strengths and weaknesses are. If it is purely acting techniques in question, then more training is needed. Besides the colleges, universities and private teachers, there are also local, more in-depth workshops on how to audition that you can take. There are also books, tapes and CDs on auditioning for your personal study. You should not take the rejection personally: if you do, you are in the wrong business. Remember, even in a small regional market, there may be 10 people who look like you, 3 people that act as well as you in your own city. Your job is to continue to train and improve so that "It" factor that is YOU comes out naturally in your auditions and makes you the best candidate. That routine you developed for after the audition? Do it again: drive, rock out in your car; go for a run; go to a movie; go hang out with non-industry friends. If you are tired, take a nap. Need to cry, cry.

What you should never do is "get crazy" on the casting team, your agent or the local actor that got the part you wanted. Watch what you say about anyone in this industry: negative energy and a nasty attitude will kill a career. Grow to the point you know you gave the best audition you could at that time and move on. Preparation + persistence + time = opportunity!

TRAINING

The Hampton Roads area of Virginia has a wide variety of training for actors. If you are seeking an academic route, there are several colleges and universities: Old Dominion, Norfolk State, Regent, Virginia Wesleyan, Tidewater Community, Thomas Nelson Community, Christopher Newport, College of William and Mary, and Hampton (Example 8). There are also community centers who give classes such as Suffolk Center of Cultural Arts.

An Internet search of Hampton Roads "acting classes" or "drama schools" will yield private teaching like Actor Keith Flippen at the Actors' Place (www.beanactor.com); Actor Mimi Eisman at Lights! Camera! Eisman (www.mimisacting.com) and Actor/Director LeRoyce Bratsveen at Iron Street Productions (www.ironstreetproductions.com). Occasionally directors, agents and theatre groups will give private lessons. They include Director Jeffrey Corriveau (www.ltnonline.org), Agent/Actor Sylvia

Hutson www.hutsontalentagency.com) and

Playwright/Director Terrance Afer-

Anderson (www.attuckstheatre.org). The

youth organizations (with classes and/or

participation for adults) include Hurrah

Players with Hugh Copeland

(www.hurrahplayers.com); Theatre for

Kids/Teens at Pembroke Mall with Grace

Atkinson (www.theaterforkidsteens.org);

Broadway Bound Academy of Theatre Arts

with Natalie Levy-Douglas and Theatrix

Productions with Kathi-Lee and Rocco

Wilson (www.theatrixproductions.com).

Ms. Hutson and Mr. Flippen have sponsored casting directors from Los Angeles, CA who hold workshops on auditioning: Tom Logan and Paul Weber. Erica Arvold of Charlottesville, VA (www.ericaarvoldcasting.com) holds a very informative workshop on "Moving and Living in LA," while Old Dominion University holds a Spring Semester in New York City. All these resources are available to you to strengthen your auditioning and acting techniques.

MONEY MATTERS

The non-union wage for most industrial videos and commercials in this area will vary from $100 to $300 to $800. The actual amount will depend on the corporate client or publicity agency you are working for. Once you join your respective union, you will make a base salary established by that union, according to which level you are being hired to. There is a level for 5 words of dialogue or less; a level for 5-10 words, and an upgraded level for supporting players with spoken interactions with the main cast.

There are set rates for the technical side, also according to that union's regulations. If you are non-union, your agent will know what the local salary rate is, and negotiate from there. For some, this is $50 an hour; for others it may be $300, $500 or more per project.

Taxes

Keep good records of your money transactions and your travel receipts. As a contractor, YOU are responsible for good records. Sometimes you are paid directly and need to pay your agent, other times the check will come from the agent. You will

damage your relationship AND your

reputation if you do not pay your agents.

When you have earned a certain amount

($600-800), you will receive a 1099-MISC

form from your agents. If paid directly from

a corporate office, you will receive a W-2

form. It is your responsibility to report ALL

acting wages during the U.S tax season.

You provide these forms to your accountant

or tax preparer. There are good tax

preparation software programs, such as

Turbo Tax©, H&R Block TaxCut© and

others, which will allow you to do your own

year-end taxes. I personally use Turbo

Tax©. The software asks questions that

allow you to plug in your numbers and does

your calculations for you. If at the end,

there is a question or concern raised, it

provides you a phone number and/or

websites to go to and resolve the problem.

If the question is more difficult, you are

directed to go to www.irs.gov for resolution.

To keep your records, use a folder, plastic

storage box, an accordion file or the audition

logbook/software. If you are keeping proper

records, you should have no problems with audits. Store your records electronically or in tax prep boxes for three years. If you are uncomfortable doing your own taxes, take your W-2s, 1099-MISCs, your receipts and your utility bill receipts to a certified public account (CPA) or a licensed tax preparer.

SCAMS

Beware of show business scams. Some will not be as obvious as others, but a lot of the entertainment business is not regulated; contracts and arrangements can be very unscrupulous. If someone asks you the performer for money upfront: **_RUN_**, don't walk, for the nearest door. This is not how legitimate acting work is done. A so-called manager or producer who arranges a meeting, then spends a lot of time "name dropping" all the famous clients he or she has worked with is a scam; especially if the

93

meeting is in a public place (restaurant, bar, club house or hotel). There are so-called acting and modeling schools that will require $2000 to enroll, supposedly to train you, provide you with your headshots/comp cards and guarantee you a contract for a movie or a project: **SCAM**. No one can guarantee you a contract. Ask to see a union affiliation certificate, a state license certificate and/or a Better Business Bureau endorsement. Ask your agent if they have worked with this organization before. Ask how long they have maintained an office in your city or the state (and from which state): some agencies move into town for 2 months, then leave. Look up the organization on the websites of the Virginia Production Alliance or the Virginia Film Office. Call the Better Business Bureau or City Chamber of Commerce and find out if the organization is listed. **Please** do not be so anxious to get work that you throw caution to the wind. There are few protections against fraud and other criminal activities like this, if you willing choose to engage in them. If you are "hired" to help them find other talent, offering to pay in cash or be paid in cash,

they are not legitimate. Read their contracts

or bring them to a lawyer for review; if

something reads fishy, it often is.

TALK STORY (Interviews)

When I lived in Honolulu, Hawaii, I learned local dialect called Hawaiian pidgin. Whenever my neighbors were inviting me over, they would say, "Come. Talk Story." I would plop down on a sofa or sit in a lawn chair and talk for hours. This chapter is that equivalent. I have asked fellow actors to contribute some reality checks into the book. Those included are strictly their opinions, although I chose what to include. Anything in parenthesis is the grammar check between me and the software.

****

I guess my biggest peeve(s) with this business (are) clients who expect us to sit at home waiting for jobs. Even if there is plenty of notice for the audition, they call us up the night before and expect us to be available for their shoot. We do have other jobs and sometimes we can't just call in sick and keep the job that helps us pay the bills. The same goes with some lighting jobs. I get called at the last minute. If they were a little more considerate about us, I'm sure we could better accommodate their needs too.

Growing old is mandatory, growing up is optional.

Phil Duffy

****

I love theatre and acting and have made some wonderful friends within the theatre community. There is a bond and sense of family that develops over the course of a production that is unlike anything else. Most of us literally "become family" and grow in love, respect and consideration. We develop the ability to "read" and anticipate one another's needs and give ourselves "artistic permission" to argue or disagree - just as a

family would or should. "Pet peeves" - I

have little patience for:

- Those who feel "entitled" to special
  consideration or "forgiveness"
  because of their art.

- Those who feel talent makes it
  somehow okay to be rude,
  inconsiderate, unkind or eccentric. (I
  don't respond well to temperamental
  artists.)

- Those who come to the rehearsal
  process unprepared and, thereby,

waste precious time. This includes

directors and performers.

Recognizing that the artistic process

evolves, I still maintain there needs to be

thorough preparation and research on the

part of all involved, especially those in

leadership positions.

Carin Cowell

In my maturity I have realized to my delight that it is not all about me, it's about the collaboration. Theatre is uniquely exciting in that the final experience of this scintillating performance art is a mystical amalgam of contributions from actors, musicians, technicians, fine artists, costumers and more. It's a creative soup that is sometimes exquisitely savory, and…yes…sometimes sour. It is a joyful privilege to be part of the process of developing the show's vision –and then experience it over and over again

with the audience! Yum!

Linda Marley Smith

Actress/Director

Actors: no reputable agent or casting

director makes you pay money up front in

order to get a job. Run; do not walk, away

from anyone who tries to.

Eileen Engel

TIPS FROM THE ROAD (Touring) - David Springstead, Sr.

1. Always check for bedbugs in your room (FIRST!)!

2. See if the hotel has laundry facilities.

3. If the answer to #2 is no, how close is the nearest Laundromat?

([I] did a 22 block round trip walk today for this!)

4. What restaurants are nearby and how expensive are they?

5. Does the hotel have a free shuttle service to run you around town?

6. Are the cable channels any good?

(The higher priced the hotel, the worse the channel selection.)

7. Is there a bar on site, and when does it close?

8. Is there a bar close by, and when does IT close?

9. Is there a massage therapist nearby, and how pricey is they?

(Especially for dancers and older folks with sore bodies.)

10. Is there a drug store nearby? (See previous reason for #9)

From Facebook: Let others lead small lives, but not you. Let others argue over small things, but not you. Let others cry over small hurts, but not you. Let others leave their future in someone else's hands, but not you.♥

Jim Rohn

This is a letter that I clipped from the 02/02/12 Edition of DragonukConnects.com.

This is Brian
Brian St. August is a Union Actor that works the NYC Market from his Baltimore MD Base

~~~~~~~~~~~~~~~~~~~~~~~~~~~~~~~~~~~

Working New York....
My daughter, actor Jaime Michaels told me years ago... New York and LA are invitation only cities. You will know when you are invited and if you are not... don't come. Over time, I grew to learn that what

Jaime meant was that you will have the kind of credits and exposure that will result in them calling you in for auditions or giving you the thumbs up concerning moving there. I had been a SAG actor working from Wilmington, NC to Philadelphia, PA with a full resume of principal roles up to and including leads in movies, TV and commercials, but I didn't really get my "invitation" to New York until I had been cast for two principal days as Sgt. McGill on "As the World Turns", by Mary Clay Boland. This was a mega casting for me because ATWT was a network soap on CBS, had an audience of 12 million and Mary Clay Boland was a two-time Emmy Award winning casting director.

Prior to that I had done a lot of work for the Investigation Discovery Channel, National Geographic and others, but my invites to NY were very few. I had acquired non-exclusive representation from Innovative Artists in NY from a training opportunity that I went to through "The Network" in NY. This got me auditions and call backs, but not a very

107

good number of either. However, once I got the "As the World Turns" gig, I found NY managers much more willing to see me. Ultimately, I auditioned for and signed with American Talent Management. Since that time, I have done a lot of commercial auditioning in NY and some dramatic work. I have booked industrials and shot in Times Square Towers.

But the reality is this… when you audition in New York; you are going against the best in the business in our half of the country. It can be intimidating at first, but soon you find that when you book your first call back, you realize that you are ready for this market and that you love the competition. This is a very competitive market and there are highly qualified people in it. If you want to vie for jobs against them you must be talented, confident, self aware and self assured. But you, most of all, MUST be very tenacious, because nothing comes easy up here. Having NY management has been positive in getting me out for many lucrative commercial roles. It hasn't proven to be that beneficial yet for dramatic roles and I am currently challenging my manager about that. I know that in LA it is really important to be in the Union. I am SAG, but I will tell you the opportunities are in NY for non-union actors, but they will quickly dissolve if you don't ultimately join SAG or AFTRA. In LA, don't even think about going out there if you aren't SAG or you won't even be considered as qualified for extra work.

One nice difference though, that I would like to point out is that I have met many, many casting directors in NY and they have generally been great... friendly, open, helpful...kind. I cannot say that about all of the casting people in the DMV at all. You may not get hired in NY, but you will be treated with respect. Every one of them has shaken my hand: Perhaps that will ring a bell with some of you in the Baltimore community. My manager told me it is because in NY, casting directors are small fish in a very big pond, but in Baltimore/Washington they are big fish in a very small pond. Consider your experiences in the DMV and see if you have had that experience sometimes. I've NEVER had a New York casting director – no matter how successful – that would not shake my hand. Emmy Winner Mary Clay Boland gives me a hug.

I am one of the unique New York talents that do not live in the City. I commute via the Megabus for auditions and bookings. My management knows where I live and they secure my auditions for times that allow me to come up to the City comfortably without being rushed once I arrive. The Megabus is about 1/5th the cost of the cheapest Amtrak train and, if you commute from Baltimore, there is no parking fee associated with the White Marsh Park and Ride. DC pickups are at Union Station. I personally enjoy the 3.5 hour ride because I get to study my sides the day of the audition without interruption.

One difference in working in New York as an actor is that most management firms and a lot of agents want exclusive contracts with you. This generally means that you will pay them their agreed upon percentage even for roles they did not lead you to booking. You also are required to "book out" whenever you are not eligible for work, such as being booked or having another commitment. This is very important, because your management or agent will submit you for roles assuming that you are available unless you tell them you are not. Managing these relationships takes care and tact. If you turn up "not available" too many times, you will find yourself having very few auditions, if any.

Personally, I really enjoy being associated with the NY market. I love establishing relationships with the casting directors and producers in the Big Apple. There is a dynamic vitality that runs through the city and the entertainment business that is very infectious. Plus, as opposed to Los Angeles which is very spread out, the New York market pretty much allows you to walk, use subways or taxis for almost everything. One day last year, I had three auditions in the same day and walked to every single one of them.

In total honesty, I must tell you that working as I do is not for everyone. Over the last two years, I have introduced a number of DMV actors to my management group and only two have stayed on. The ones that did not stay on, gave up the whole idea of finding other NY management and just felt that it was too far or too frustrating. Incidentally, finding management is like finding a job: You are much more desirable when you have management than when you don't. Let that be a word to the wise. Secondly, you really MUST manage your relationships so that a degree of equality exists. They will have demands of you and you can have demands of them as well. Every year, I sit and discuss my career objectives with my manager and then monitor our progress throughout the year.

If you are an actor committed to succeeding in this business, I highly encourage you to investigate the possibility of working in NY. You will see your skills grow by being exposed to very talented competition and you will often find yourself auditioning against people you are used to seeing in Network episodics and commercials.

Whatever you do, I wish you the best. There is always a place for another great actor... you just have to let them know that you are the one!

Brian St. August

Here is another clipping from the 02/25/12 www.DragonukConnects.com Newsletter

This is the 3rd Story from Local (Baltimore/Washington DC Area) Actors working the NYC market

When "The Brian" [Dragonuk] asks me to do something, the answer isn't either "Yes" or "No", it's "When do you need it?" I confess, I procrastinated for a few weeks and here I sit staying up all night waiting for my 3:00am call time. Ah, the glamorous life.

If you want to try New York City (NYC), you can always get a cheap sublet and stay for a few months, there's couchsurfing.org, they have a group called NYC Rents and Sublets, I'm sure there are other related websites too along with good old craigslist. This way you get to network with other actors and the casting agencies get to know you as well. If you're used to being a big fish in a little pond then you're in for a shock. You're going to be a microscopic algae in a vast ocean - Just Kidding, it's not that bad. There are approximately 100,000 actors in the greater New York City area so it's highly competitive.

Almost everyone I know that does background (BG) work is a member of www.CastingNetworks.com. It's about you and your headshot. One of my friends told me that the Casting Directors don't even look at your resume; they look at your headshot and your union status.

You can register with the casting agencies directly to be in their personal databases. Casting Networks.com is a third party consolidator. The big ones are Grant Wilfley and Central Casting.com ($25 non-refundable fee). Why would you register with each one individually? Because they call you first and then when they have extra slots to fill they use a 3rd party (like CastingNetworks.com) and it's usually either a day or two after they call you that you'll see the casting show up on Casting Networks.com.

A little bit about me and how I got started. I started out as a commercial model and then an Independent Film Director contacted me through one of the modeling websites (I'm on ModelMayhem.com and OneModelPlace.com) and asked me if I would be interested in being in his film.

Wow, a challenge, it's like "She has a good look, now let's see if she can walk and talk at the same time." That was in 2004, I've been doing acting and modeling ever since. I saw a casting call on one of the modeling website for an Asian female for a drug store chain and I submitted my picture and I got it! (Non-union gig), my image has been around as the Duane Reade Pharmacist since April 2009. It's fun when people recognize me. However, I have to admit that I have a twin who looks more like me than me. She gets stopped almost daily and people ask her if she's me. ROR raffing out roud.

I try to network like crazy with other actors and models when I'm working. I consider it a failure if I haven't handed my actor business card to at least one new person. You never know who will help you along the way in your career. I also believe in sharing and good karma.

I contribute to the DragonukConnects.com job postings, about ⅔ of my contributions make it into the newsletter. Some of the postings have resulted in paid work for my fellow actors, so I'm told. That makes me very happy. I ask other actors about agencies and websites and they come to me when they have questions too. It's all about sharing, it's not about you. There's one background agency, which will remain nameless that charges a monthly fee and they get you work in the beginning but then they stop and still expect you to pay them each month. There's a Manager who's a bit shady, according to a trustworthy source so I have stayed away from that Manager. I'm proud to say that I got peeps, people who watch my back and I've got their backs.

It's always good to get your training and make your mistakes in the smaller markets like DC, Baltimore, etc. then when you come to work in New York, you'll already be very professional. I prefer to take things in baby steps, I started traveling to NYC and I would stay for 3 days in a row, then it got to be 5 days of working, go sees and auditions. So I thought it was time to finally move here. I'm currently in a modest sublet in Chinatown and enjoying my red bean bun and coffee for two dollah every morning.

You'll find your niche, mine is the Nerdy
Asian Female/Professional woman, which is
fine with me. Some people get lucky and
have a big success immediately; others get
steady background work 2-3 days per week
and are content. Continue to hone your craft,
whatever it may be; there are many
opportunities and networking groups.
There's an Asian Film Lab that I learned
about recently, there's Actors Connection,
HB Studio, The Actors Fund, Fractured
Atlas and I'm sure numerous others on
LinkedIn and elsewhere in person and on the
web. Finally, don't forget about craigslist
nyc, you have to put your filter up to weed
out the scams but there are genuine
opportunities out there. Maybe create a
separate email address just for replies to
craigslist posts. I booked a non-union acting
job on craigslist in DC a few years ago that
paid $1,200 for an airline contractor in
Virginia so you never know. I just worked a
launch party during New York's Fashion
Week (NYFW) which is closed to the
general public that I got off craigslist.
Shweet.

Many actors also do promotional modeling jobs, usually live events, there are many national companies that work in the NYC area, you just have to register with each one, create your profile and upload your photos. There's also one company that books talent for events at the Javits Center, like the registration table, etc. Ok, my time is up, I gotta get ready and walk to the subway at 1:30am, ugh, can't miss that courtesy van, otherwise I'll be in deep doo doo.

Peace & Love,
Lil Rhee
February 21, 2012

THE LAST WORD

I can just hear you. "This was a really cool book, but you forgot this …"

Go back and look at the title. Lessons learned so far. My lessons in Hampton Roads have been as varied as the population and the cultures of the area. When I first was stationed here, I knew I could "home-base" here. There were so many playhouses to choose from and so much independent filmmaking going on, I made a personal goal to work as much as possible while I lived here.

When I answered my first film call, I was excited to see if I had those chops, too. After a couple of classes and several extra roles, I felt myself growing in this arena, too. I am really proud of my supporting and featured roles, as well as my principal ones. Even the technical opportunities came along in the areas of production assisting, screenwriting, casting and directing.

So what am I trying to say?

If it is your dream, go for it. Just because you are older, does not mean you have to change, stop dreaming or give up everything

to younger people.

Go on. Get out there. Break a leg.

ACKNOWLEDGEMENTS

Thank you, Sylvia Hutson. You have been my "best" agent and one of my best friends for a long time. You have shown me in so many ways how much you trust me as an actor and as a friend. There is so much I couldn't do without you.

Thanks, Matthew Friedman and Angela Best. You guys are always telling me to just sit down and write. I finally did.

Thank you, LeRoyce Braatsveen. It's not always easy for us strong women, you know that. I have the utmost respect for what you've accomplished and the inspiration I get from you. Thanks for the advice.

Thank you, Terrell Dean. As I began to answer your questions, I realized I needed to go ahead and start this book.

Thank you to my "Talk Story" contributors: Phil Duffy, Carin Cowell, Linda Marley Smith, Eileen Engel, David Springstead, Sr. and Brian Dragonuk. Your "pearls of wisdom" are greatly appreciated.

Thank you, Brad Rudacille, Francine Humphreys and Bob O'Donnell, for directing me to good self-publishing sites. It was frustrating to choose one but it was

good advice!

Thank you, Rona Hyman, for catching

misspelled words!

HAMPTON ROADS, VIRGINIA – Places of Interest (Smithfield, Suffolk, Chesapeake, Virginia Beach, Norfolk, Hampton, Newport News, and Williamsburg)

Suffolk Cultural Arts Center
110 W. Finney Avenue
Suffolk, VA 23434
(757) 923-0003

Smithfield Little Theater
210 N. Church St.
Smithfield, VA 23430
(757) 357-7338

The New Theatre of Chesapeake
P.O. Box 2276
Chesapeake, VA 23327

Little Theatre of Virginia Beach
550 Barberton Drive
Virginia Beach, VA 23451
(757) 428-9233

Virginia Musical Theater
Sandler Center for the Performing Arts
201 Market Street
Virginia Beach, Virginia 23462
(757) 385-2555

Light Opera of Virginia Beach
Sandler Center for the Performing Arts
201 Market Street
Virginia Beach, Virginia 23462
(757) 385-2555

Little Theatre of Norfolk
801 Claremont Ave
Norfolk, VA 23507
(757) 627-8551

Generic Theater
215 St. Paul's Blvd
Norfolk, VA 23510
(757) 441-2160

Wells Theater
108 East Tazewell Street
Norfolk, VA 23510
(757) 627-6988

The Venue at 35th Street
631 35th Street
Norfolk, VA 23508
(757) 469-0337

The Roper Theater at Tidewater Community
College Norfolk
340 Granby Street
Norfolk VA 23510
(757) 822-1450

Hurrah Players
485 St Pauls Blvd
Norfolk, VA 23510
(757) 627-5437

The Attucks Theater
1010 Church Street
Norfolk, VA 23504
(757) 622-4763

The American Theater
125 East Mellen Street
Hampton, VA 23663
(757) 722-2787

Iron Street Productions
122 Virginia Lane
Yorktown, VA 23693
(757) 969-1419

Virginia Opera and Symphony
160 East Virginia Beach Blvd
Norfolk, VA 23510
(757) 627-9545

Virginia Governor's School of the Arts
1542 West 49th Street
Norfolk, VA 23508
(757) 451-4711

Theater for Kids/Teens!
219-A 70th St.
Virginia Beach, VA
(757)425-1445

Theatrix Productions, Inc.
821 Sunnyside Drive, Suite L
Virginia Beach, VA 23464
(757)523-0876

INDEX

Example 1 – Headshot

Example 2 – Resume

Example 3 – Tech Resume

Example 4 – Business Card

Example 5 – Tools of the Trade

Example 6 – Websites and Social Media

Example 7 – Local hangouts

Example 8 - Colleges and Universities

Example 9 - Photographers

Example 1 – Headshots

Cynthia Tademy

Cynthia Tademy

Example 2 – Resume

Cynthia Tademy

Height: 5'10"   Weight: Plus
Hair: Short, Salt/Pepper, Braids Eyes: Brown
Hutson Talent Agency 757.xxx.xxxx

Selected Films

Lemon and Tea	Principal	Regent Pictures
Conspiracy Nation	Principal	Cine-magic Video Prod.
Cycle	Principal	Reel Vision Prod.
All in the Name of God	Sup. Player	Diamond Film Co.
Flowers	Principal	Regent Pictures
Rock-Paper-Scissors	Feat. Player	Regent Pictures

Commercials

Priority Toyota	Nun	Ritz Marketing
Carepoint Shoes	Girlfriend	Carepoint
VA PSA	Grandmother	Park Group
Go Red– Heart Assoc.	Principal	The Syndicate

Theater

Hairspray	M. Maybelle	Newport News, VA
Ladies First	Hannah	Norfolk, VA
Working	Maggie	Norfolk, VA
Ain't Misbehavin'	Nell Carter Songs	Norfolk, VA
A Raisin in the Sun	Mama	Newport News, VA

Training

Act Workshops	T. Logan, P. Weber	VA Beach, VA
Meisner Technique	Keith Flippen	VA Beach, VA
UCI	BFA - Drama	Irvine, CA

Special Skills: Whoopi Lookalike; Alto/Tenor; W. Indian/Jamaican accents; Bowling; Full-Figure Model; US Navy Vet; V-O; MC/Hostess; Production Assistant; Stage Director; Film Development/Screenwriter.

Example 3

CYNTHIA TADEMY
Technical Resume for Stage/Film
Email: ctademy@gmail.com
757-xxx-xxxx

Professional Experience:

Conspiracy: 7 Cities   Chris Abaya Productions
Admin. Asst.
November Shorts 2010   Venue at 35th Street
Director, Casting
No Place Like Home (Webisodes)Black Onyx
Productions/Line Producer, Screenwriter
Trial of Short-Sighted Woman   Venue at 35th Street
Actor, Director
The Miracle Worker   LTN
Director
The Man Who Came To Dinner   LTN
Asst. Director
A Raisin in the Sun   PCT
Actor, Asst. Dir.

Little Theatre of Norfolk   Board of Directors
                                   Publicity/Marketing

References available upon request

Example 4 – Business Cards

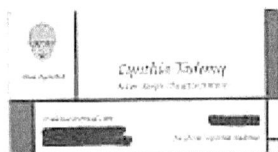

136

Example 5 – Tools of the Trade

*Headshots
*Resumes
*Business Cards/Comp Cards
*Car/Truck/SUV
*Cell/smart phone/GPS
Demo Reels/videos
* Actor Bag/Box (in vehicle)
        Charger (ipod, cell, laptop, etc)
        Comb, brush, hairspray
        Cough drops/throat spray (Singers)
        Deodorant, toothbrush, toothpaste
        Emery board, clippers
        Extra contacts/glasses/sunglasses
        Extra headshots
        Extra resumes
        Facial tissue, wet and dry
        Makeup
        Mints
        Pain reliever
        Pantyhose
        Post-it Notes
        Safety Pins
        Sharpies, pens, pencils
        Small mirror
        Stapler/glue stick
        Wigs/hat/black shoes
Computer/laptop/tablet
Log book/software
Website/webpage
Thank You cards/notes/stamps

*Essential items

Example 6

WEBSITES AND SOCIAL MEDIA
(Suggested)

48hrFilms.com
78hrFilms.com
800Casting.con
ActorsAccess.com
ActorsTips.com
Attucks.com
BackStageWest.com
Breakdownservices.com
BranchOut.com
Box.com
CentralCasting.com
Craigslist.com
Dragonout Newsletter
DailyVariety.com
Facebook.com
FilmmakersMagazine.com
HeeryCasting.com
JaderlundCasting.com
LinkedIn.com
LiquidTalent.com
MikeLemonCasting.com

Modelogic.com
MySpace.com
NOWCasting.com
Oldies.com
PatMoran.com
SpencerandAssociates.com
Talent-Link.com
Twitter.com
UptownTalent.com
Vimeo.com
VirginiaActorsForum.com
VirginiaFilmOffice.com
VirginiaProductionAlliance.com
Vistaprints.com
Youtube.com

Example 7

LOCAL HANGOUTS

VA Beach Town Center (P.F. Chang's; The
Cheesecake Factory; Zushi)
222 Central Park Avenue
Virginia Beach, VA

Panera Bread
739 West 21st Street
Norfolk, VA
(757) 623-9669

California Pizza Kitchen
222 Central Park Avenue
The Town Center of Virginia Beach
Virginia Beach, VA
(757) 456-2630

Gordon Biersch Brewery Restaurant
4561 Virginia Beach Boulevard
Virginia Beach, VA
The Town Center of Virginia Beach
(757) 490-2739

The Funny Bone
217 Central Park Avenue
Virginia Beach, VA
The Town Center of Virginia Beach
(757) 213-5555

Cozzy's Comedy Club & Tavern
9700 Warwick Boulevard
Newport News, VA
Hilton Shopping Center
(757) 595-2800

Belmont Smoke Café
2117 Colonial Avenue
Norfolk, VA
(757) 623-4477

Joe's Crab Shack
333 Waterside Dr
Norfolk, VA
Waterside Festival Marketplace
(757) 625-0655

Hell's Kitchen
124 Granby Street
Norfolk, VA
(757) 624-1906

Starbucks (Various Locations)
Chesapeake, VA
Norfolk, VA
Virginia Beach, VA

Kelly's Tavern
1408 Colley Ave
Norfolk, VA
(757) 623-3216

Kelly's Tavern
1936 Laskin Rd # 201
Virginia Beach, VA
Regency Hilltop Shopping Center
(757) 491-8737

Naro Cinema and Video Store
1507 Colley Avenue
Norfolk, VA
(757) 625-6276

Kerouac Café
617 W 35th St
Norfolk, VA
(757) 625-8600

Fair Grounds
806 Baldwin Avenue # 2
Norfolk, VA 23517
(757) 640-2899

IHOP Restaurant
114 East 21st Street
Norfolk, VA
(757) 625-2866

Mambo Room
2200 Colonial Avenue # 4
Norfolk, VA
(757) 351-6092

No Frill Bar & Grill
806 Spotswood Avenue
Norfolk, VA
(757) 627-4262

Cogan's Pizza
1901 Colonial Avenue
Norfolk, VA
(757) 627-6428

Cruzers Seaman's Club (karaoke)
601 Orapax Street
Norfolk, VA
(757) 622-3004

Tortilla West Bar
508 Orapax Street
 Norfolk, VA
(757) 440-3777

Wanna B's   (karaoke)
2880 Virginia Beach Boulevard
Virginia Beach, VA
Lynnhaven Shopping Center
(757) 340-5671

The Palace on Plume
200 E. Plume Street
Norfolk, VA
(757) 962-2135

Example 8

COLLEGES/UNIVERSITIES

Christopher Newport University	www.cnu.edu
College of William and Mary	www.wm.edu
Norfolk State University	www.nsu.edu
Old Dominion University	www.odu.edu
Regent University	www.regent.edu
T. Nelson Community College	www.tnccc.edu
Tidewater Community College	www.tcc.edu
Virginia Wesleyan College	www.vwc.edu

Example 9

PHOTOGRAPHERS

Dustin Lewis
www.DustinLewisImages.com
Virginia Beach, VA
(757) 748-2586

Melissa Blue
www.MelissaBluePhoto.com
Hampton Roads, VA

Pam Manning
www.TheManningStudio.com
Norfolk, VA
(757) 623-7888

Angela Best
Portsmouth, VA
www.facebook.com/Angela.Best

Paul Costen
Norfolk, VA
www.facebook.com/Paul.Costen

David Beloff
David Adam Beloff Photography
www.dabphotos.com
(757) 617-2266

Brad Rudacille
Rudacille & Design
www.brpix.com
(757) 343-3067

Keith Cephus
Keith Cephus Photography
www.keithcephus.com
(757) 430-2169

Marilen Sarian
Art Inspired
www.artinspired.com
(757) 768-9033

Brett Moye
(757) 513-0724

RECOMMENDED BOOKS

7 Roles Every Actor Must Play – Leslie Becker

Acting in the Million Dollar Minute – Tom Logan

Acting Qs: Conversations with Working Actors –
Bonnie Gillespie

An Actor Succeeds: Career Management for the
Actor – Terrance Hines and Suzanne Vaughn

Casting Qs: A Collection of Casting Director
Interviews – Bonnie Gillespie

How To Act & Eat at the Same Time – Tom Logan

How To Sell Yourself As An Actor – K Callan

One Less Bitter Actor – Markus Flanagan

Self-Management for Actors: Getting to Show

Business – Bonnie Gillespie (Highly Recommended!)

The Business of Acting – Brad Lemack

The Cabaret Artist's Handbook – Bob Harrinton

The Hollywood Rules – Anonymous

BIOGRAPHY

Cynthia Tademy

Cynthia Harris Tademy is a well-known actor/director in the Hampton Roads, VA area. She debuted on the big screen in original, award-winning film shorts *FLOWERS* and *RPS* (Rock-Paper-Scissors) with Regent University Productions. Cynthia also appeared in the short film, *CYCLE,* which won the Audience Choice Award at the 2008 Mid-Atlantic Film Festival, Norfolk, VA. She performed at the Generic Theater (Norfolk) in that theater's final production on 21st Street, *Ain't Misbehavin'*. When the Generic moved to the Chrysler Hall location in 2010, she performed in Roald Dahl's *The Witches*. Other Hampton Roads theaters Cynthia has performed for are Theatrix Productions, The Hurrah Players, Little Theatre of Norfolk, Little Theatre of VA Beach and Peninsula Community Theater, Newport News. She directed *The Miracle Worker* for the Little Theatre of Norfolk. She earned her BFA in Drama from the University of California – Irvine and is a United States Navy retiree. Cynthia lives in Virginia Beach, VA and has 2 loving brothers, sisters-in-laws; loads of nieces, nephews, cousins and a cat named Lilo.

www.ingramcontent.com/pod-product-compliance
Lightning Source LLC
LaVergne TN
LVHW021500080426
835509LV00018B/2349